C0-BLD-494

GOD THOUGHTS FROM A FARMER'S DAUGHTER

TANIA WALL

ISBN 978-1-64114-295-3 (Paperback)
ISBN 978-1-64114-296-0 (Digital)

Copyright © 2017 by Tania Wall
All rights reserved. No part of this publication may be reproduced, distributed, or transmitted in any form or by any means, including photocopying, recording, or other electronic or mechanical methods without the prior written permission of the publisher. For permission requests, solicit the publisher via the address below.

Christian Faith Publishing, Inc.
296 Chestnut Street
Meadville, PA 16335
www.christianfaithpublishing.com

Printed in the United States of America

DEDICATION

This book is dedicated to my Father in heaven, he is my teacher and mentor, for his wonderful and amazing love for me and for saving my life. I also dedicate this book to my family for all their love and support through the years.

CONTENTS

INTRODUCTION

My life on the dairy farm was hard work. Our families raised most of our own food and feed for the cows. We raised our own replacement heifers. So there was always a lot happening around the farm.

I learned so much on the farm feeding calves, milking the cows and helped harvesting the hay. All this time on the farm, it has made me the person I am today. When I found the Lord, I was like a newborn calf that found mother's milk for the first time and wanted more. I wanted to do more for God. I didn't know how until God showed me. These are my life stories that helped me and that could help others.

DIRTY SPOTS

When I was a little kid, one of my chores was to clean Dad's equipment. I especially remember cleaning the hay baler, by hosing it. I was so proud of myself and called out to Dad, "Look how good a job I did!" Balers have lots of nooks and crannies and are not easy to clean. Dad would show me an area that was still dirty. I'd do it again and might get another "you missed this spot" from Dad. More hosing. How thrilled I would be to finally get Dad's "It's all clean. Good job!"

Later, when in my twenties, when I was cleaning the baler, I remembered trying to clean the baler when I was a kid. The thought came to me that God is telling us there are dirty spots in our lives. We need to clean them good so people can't point to the dirty spots. We need to know all the dirty spots are clean.

God is like Dad, pointing out the spots we need to clean. He does that through His Holy Spirit and His Word.

"Search me, O God, and know my heart; test me and know my anxious thoughts. See if there is any offensive way in me, and lead me in the way everlasting" (Ps. 139:23–24).

> "If we confess our sins, he is faithful and just and will forgive as our sins and purify as from all unrighteousness" (1 John 1:9).

The Baler I cleaned after hay season was over.

CORN MAZE

When I was about five years old, I wanted to be just like my dad and do everything he did on the farm. Our parents knew how much we liked living on the farm and so when they gave us toys, they were ones we really liked. One time, they gave us all toy tractors. They were not just plastic toys, but real metal ones that probably weighed about five pounds. I was so little that I couldn't carry mine around. So once when Dad went out to the field to work, he took me along and carried my tractor for me. He put me and the tractor next to the cornfield while he worked. He told me to stay there and play with my little orange tractor until he returned in a few minutes. "Okay, Daddy," I said. And he left. It seemed like I waited forever for him to return. I finally decided to go look for him, maybe hear his voice and follow the sound. I started into the cornfield, but soon realized that that was a mistake. I had no idea which way to go, or even which way I had come. I wandered aimlessly, in and out of muddy areas, hoping to hear his voice. I remembered that we were always told to pray when we needed help. So I stood there and prayed to God to get me out of the cornfield. Then I also remembered Dad telling us one time that if you are ever lost in a cornfield, just walk a straight line and you will reach the edge eventually. So I did that, and sure enough, I found myself on the other side of the cornfield. I knew I needed to be on the other side, so I turned around and walked straight back the way I had come to get to the side where my little orange tractor was. Finally, I did make it to the tractor, and there was my dad. He wasn't mad, but glad that I remembered what he had told me and that I had found my way back again. I think that's how God is—always there for us.

In Proverbs 3:6, we read, *"Trust in the Lord with all your heart and lean not on your own understanding; in all your ways acknowledge Him, and He will make your paths straight."*

The cornfield on our farm.

EATING VEGETABLES WHILE EYING CHOCOLATE CAKE!

We know we should eat vegetables—after all, they are good for us, they make us feel good, they contain good nutrition for us. But we look at the cake and think how delicious it would be—all that sugar! All that frosting! All that sweet filling! That's how it is with people. They see God as Someone that they know is good for them. But the way the world lives is so much more intriguing to them even though it is not good for them. They know God is better for them, but the things of the world are so tempting. The Bible has a solution…

> *"No temptation has seized you except what is common to man. And God is faithful; he will not let you be tempted beyond what you can hear. But when you are tempted, he will also provide a way out so that you can stand up under it" (1 Cor. 10:13, NIV).*

My dinner one night yum vegetables.

LUCKY

When we were little kids, we found out how lucky we were to be who we were, having the parents we did and having the life we did on the farm. My parents got us some tapes—sixty-four of them were Bible stories, and sixty-four were character-building tapes to help us become better people. In one of the tapes, there was a story about this little girl who didn't have very much money. She wanted to go to school but didn't have the money, so she picked blackberries in her bare feet (because she didn't have any shoes). She would take the berries to someone she hoped would send her to school.

Jason and I thought that was a good idea. So one day, we went out to the blackberry patches barefoot and picked berries just to see how she would have felt, not having shoes. It was a painful experience! But it was an experience we valued because it helped us realize how "lucky" we were to have what we had.

My mother told us that day when we got home, barefoot and dirty-handed, that we looked like little orphan children! So we told her why we had done it and how we wanted to experience what the little girl in the story did.

Sometimes, in order to understand how another person feels, we need to "experience" it ourselves. That way, we can better understand what they are going through. And sometimes, God allows us to go through something, and we don't understand why. Perhaps, He is allowing us to go through it so we can be more understanding or helpful when we meet someone else going through the same thing. This may give you the opportunity to explain how the love of God that you have in your heart helped you go through the same experience. We need to be open to letting God teach us in the bad times.

WANTING MORE

When my dad would lose something, he would always ask us kids to come help him find it. It might be his wallet, car keys, glasses—all different types of things. As we got older, he'd even give us a reward if we found it. At first, it would be some loose change; later, it might even be a dollar. My brothers saw this as a great opportunity to make a little cash. So, when they expected him to be looking for something, they'd pick it up and hold onto it. Then when Dad would ask, "Do you know where my _____ is?" They would say, "How much will you give if we find it?" If they didn't think it was enough, they might say, "But don't you need it now?" This would drive the price up further and finally they would settle on a "fair" price. Then, of course, they would find it quickly and claim their reward. Dad, however, soon figured them out and stopped offering rewards! And because he knew I wasn't demanding a reward, he soon would just call out, "Tania, where's this? Where's that? Tania, I can't find…!"

It seems we always want more—more clothes, more food, more money, more "toys", more attention, or a bigger house. But God tells us to be content with what we have. This is found in Hebrews 13:5.

> *"Keep your lives free from the love of money and be content with what you have, because God has said, 'Never will I leave you; never will I forsake you.'"*

OLD CARS

My brother Frank likes to work on old cars. He will bring home an old car and say, "Look what I found for a good deal! Don't you think it is beautiful?" And we look at it and say that maybe it was when it was new. We only see how much work needs to be done on it. The seats may be chewed by mice; it may have a lot of rust all over it; and maybe it doesn't even run.

I ask my brother, as he is hosing and cleaning one of his old cars, "How can you see so much in this dirty old car?" He just wonders why we can't see what he does. He looks at a car and sees what it will look like when he is done restoring it. This is what drives him to keep finding old cars to fix up. He sees something that we don't. He knows they will run again one day when he is done working on them. He sees the finished product on the road!

I was thinking that just like what my brother sees in his old cars, God sees in us. He sees what we will become before anyone else can. God sees our future after we are cleaned up and "on the road".

> *"For I know the plans I have for you, declares the Lord, plans to prosper you and not to harm you, plans to give you hope and a future" (Jer. 29:11, NIV).*

My dad pulling one of my brother's old cars a round.

COW MAGNETS

Strong magnets, the size of your index finger, are pushed down the throats of heifers with a special pusher. These stay in the stomachs of the cows for life. They attract the metallic items that cows eat accidentally (nails, pieces of wire, staples, etc.) and keep them from passing into the intestines and injuring or killing the cow.

God is like a magnet to take the bad things away so we can be clean and safe and be used for Him. Bad things allowed to follow their natural course in our lives lead to bad consequences. God tells us that we can be cleansed of our bad things (sin) by confessing them to Him and turning from them.

> *"If we confess our sins He is faithful and just to forgive us our sins and to cleanse us from all unrighteousness" (1 John 1:9).*

Some of our Holstein heifers hanging out at the barn.

LOOKING ON

When a little baby calf is in trouble, stuck in the muck in the pasture, unable to get free, the mother is unable to do anything to help; she doesn't have arms and legs like we do. The only thing she has that she can use is her head, but pushing her baby with her head would probably only make things worse. She knows that her only hope is that the farmer will see the situation and come to help. All she can do is look helplessly on while her baby sinks deeper into the mud. This made me think about how mothers of teenage kids must feel sometimes. They pray for them and do the best they can for them and maybe even wish that they had been able to do more. Yet, the choices the kids make may get them stuck in a bad situation that the mother can do nothing about, but look on and pray that God will intervene and help the child. The mother has to just trust God to act on their behalf in His timing.

Unlike the mother cow, God can do more than just look on. He not only sees us in our distresses, but He also has the power to deliver us.

"From Heaven the LORD *looks down and sees all mankind; from His dwelling place He watches all who live on the earth"* (Ps. 33:14–15).

IN THE LIGHT

One of my teenage responsibilities was to clean my great-aunt Martha's house once a week. Mom would take me there, and I would do light housekeeping for her—sweeping, dusting, mopping, etc.

I remember one particularly dark, rainy Oregon day when I was sweeping the kitchen. For some reason, I didn't turn the light on but worked in the dim light. When I finished sweeping, I was having trouble seeing to get the sweepings into the dustpan so I turned on the light. When I could see it all, I was amazed how much dirt I had swept up! And I knew it would have horrified my "Mennonite" auntie!

I couldn't help but think of how much like that our lives are. We don't realize sometimes how much "dirt" there is in our lives, until God "turns the light on" by revealing it to us through His Word.

Also, we don't know how much we have "touched" others, unless God chooses to reveal it to us.

> *"The unfolding of your words gives light" (Ps. 119:130). "For God, who said, 'Let light shine out of darkness, made his light shine in our hearts to give us the light of the knowledge of the glory of God in the face of Christ'" (2 Cor. 4:6).*

CATS!

I grew up on a dairy farm. Some people assume that if they had a cat they didn't want, they dairy people would take it—after all, they have milk. Every once in a while, someone would drop off a cat at our farm. Because we had so many cats, we wanted to do an experiment we had heard about that other people had done. We wanted to see if it was true and if we could actually do it.

Every once in a while, when we kids were milking in the barn, a cat would wander through. We'd call it, "Here, kitty, kitty." We'd try to spray milk from the cow directly into the cat's mouth. Most of them would make a dash for the door; some would just look at us as if to say, *What are you doing?* and some would actually act indignant. But there was this one cat that would take her paw, rub the milk off her face and lick it. So at least one cat got some milk from our experiment. We thought it pretty "cool" to have tried it.

I was thinking about young Christians. They may want to try out things—to see what happens. They may want to know if what they have been told is true. They may try some things in their attempt to learn things, just like us little kids did.

Just like cats and little kittens thrive on milk, so as the newborn baby. *The Bible tells us in 1 Peter 2:2, "Like new born babies, crave pure spiritual milk, so that by it you may grow up in your salvation, now that you have tasted that the Lord is good." We get that "spiritual milk" by reading the Word of God.*

Some of our kittens on the farm.

GOD'S LOVE

My mom got very sick when I was about thirteen. A number of churches prayed for her during this time. When she was better, she said that we needed to go around to these churches and thank them for praying. So for several weeks, we went to a different church every Sunday in order to thank them.

The one church where I felt the most love was in Waldport. We walked in there, and we felt welcome. We felt we could come in, sit down, and relax. In some of the other churches, we felt we were being looked at critically.

The feeling that should be felt in a church is that "God loves you." When this is what you feel, then this is a place you don't want to leave—a place you want to come back to.

We need to show visitors love. Show them that God loves them. Greet them. Say a kind word. Do something to show them that they are loved. *Jesus said in John 13:34–35: "A new commandment I give you, that you love one another as I have loved you, that you also love one another. By this shall all men know that you are my disciples, if you have love to one another."*

MOST IMPORTANT GIFT

I remember when I was little, when we'd get up on Christmas Day and go downstairs and see the Christmas tree with all the presents under it, we'd be so excited. But my mother would always say, "Before we open presents, we have to read the Christmas story so you will understand the true meaning of Christmas. But even before we do that, we have to wait for your father to get in from milking, and we have to get all our chores done and have breakfast." We'd do our chores as fast as we could and eat breakfast as fast as we could, but we'd have to wait till everyone was done. Finally, we'd be done and could go into the living room. Mom would have Dad sit in his chair with us around him. He would read the story to us. And he would tell us the lights on the Christmas tree were to remind us of the star that shone to announce the day that Jesus was born. The presents under the tree reminded us of the gifts that the magi brought to Jesus. These were all reminders of God's grace in giving us His only Son. I tried to remember all these things as I got older.

When we were little, the first gifts we'd open would often be toys. Later on, the gifts became more practical, like the Christmas when I got my first pair of insulated coveralls. It was so good to wear them in the cold barn when I was milking. But the most important gift of Christmas is the gift God gave us.

> *"For it is by grace you have been saved, through faith—and this is not of yourselves, it is the gift of God not by works, so that no one can boast" (Eph. 2:8–9).*

GOD LOVES ME

It was hard for me when my favorite cat died. As the years went by, I thought it would be so neat to have a cat that was from one of her kittens. At that time, I only knew of two—one was fixed and the other one never had any kittens. Her only male kitten had run off years ago when we got a dog.

So I prayed and asked God that if it was His will, that I would find a cat that looked like her and came from her family. One day, I went out to the field walking to work and saw Oreo go after something. When I got to where he was, I found out it was a cat hiding in Dad's old pickup trying to get away from the dog. As I looked around, I saw a kitten in the tall grass. The kitten looked just like my old cat! So I picked her up to keep her safe from the dog.

When I got home, I told my dad to look at what I found. He said, "Not another cat!" I said yes, but this one looked just like my cat that died. He said that since it looked so much like my old cat, I could keep it. Each time I look at her, I am reminded of how much God loves me—to answer my prayer and give me a cat that looks like the one that died.

The Lord answered my prayers. I can say, like the psalmist, *"I love the Lord because He heard my voice and my supplications; therefore will I call upon Him as long as I live"* (Ps. 116:1–2).

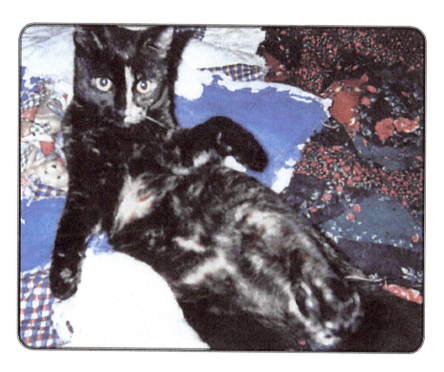

My cat paddles.

BRINGING IN THE EGGS

One of my jobs on the farm was to gather up the eggs. One day, when I was gathering them, one slipped out of the basket and broke. The chickens went nuts over that egg, gathering around to feast on it! I took the rest into the house to prepare them to sell by washing them. In that process, another one broke. I put the rest safely into the carton. When you think about it, every broken egg is money lost. The money made from the sale of the eggs goes for the purchase of the chickens, their feed, and maintenance. So any broken eggs are a great loss. God does the same thing with us. He gathers us up to Himself. Some of us will break away and fall down, and Satan will feast upon us. Others of us, under the pressure of being made clean by God, will also break. Some of us will "make it to the carton" and do what God intends for us to do. Every one He loses, hurts. It is one less person to serve Him and help in His work. That's what I think of when an egg breaks.

"Your Father in heaven is not willing that any of these little ones should be lost" (Matt. 18:14, NIV).

The egg nest where the chicken laid their eggs in.

BABY CALF STUCK

I was going out to feed the cows one day and I noticed a baby calf was stuck in the muck and couldn't get out. I contemplated the situation and realized there were two ways to thinking about it. I could have just said, "Yuck, I don't want to go out there into that messy pasture. Maybe he'll get out on his own eventually." Or I could just go to where he was and try to get him out. I decided to go in and help him, but getting there was a real challenge. It felt like I had suction cups on my feet, sucking me into the muck. But I kept going. I was wondering how I'd get out if I got stuck in there. But I kept going and got to him. I prayed for help in getting him out. With God's help, I had enough strength to pull him free of the suction. I got him back to his mother, who had only been helplessly watching.

We, sometimes, get stuck in life. We make a wrong choice and get stuck. Our feet just won't move. The only hope we have is to trust in God and to pray to Him to get us unstuck! He can help us do what our feet are supposed to do—to follow Him. He needs us to be His hands and His feet and serve Him.

I am reminded of what the psalmist said:

> "I waited patiently for the LORD; He turned to me and heard my cry. He lifted me out of the slimy pit, out of the mud and mire; He set my feet on a rock and gave me a firm place to stand. He put a new song in my mouth, a hymn of praise to our God" (Ps. 40:1–3, NIV).

One of our calves.

BRINGING IN THE COWS

One of our jobs as kids on the dairy was to get all the cows from the field or pasture down to the milking parlor by a certain time so they could be milked. We had to watch out for cows that had a calf. Once, we noticed that a cow was acting like she had a calf after she got to the barn. So my brother and I went back out to the pasture to see if we could find her calf. When we got to the part of the field where we thought it might be, we saw a coyote lurking around. We made a lot of noise and scared him off. We assumed that he had gotten the calf, and it was a goner. But we continued looking and did find the calf, lying still on the ground. When we got closer, we realized that it was still breathing. We gave it the bottle we had with us, and it drank the whole thing and then followed us back home.

I was thinking that so often when dangers are around us and we feel hopeless, that God is there to protect us. He even uses His angels, like the psalmist says in Psalm 91:11, *"For He will command His angels concerning you to guard you in all your ways, they will lift you up in their hands so that you will not strike your foot against a stone."*

Getting the cows in for milking.

JUST LIKE DAD

When I was little, I always wanted so much to be just like my dad. I knew that when it would be time for me to get a husband, I wanted him to be just like my dad.

Dad came to breakfast one day wearing his shirt inside out. I asked him why he was doing that. He replied that by doing that, he could wear it four times before having to get a clean one—he could wear it front and back, then inside out front and back!

Whenever my grandmother came over, I always had to change my shirt so I would look clean to her. We were often dirty from chores, and my mother wanted us to look our best for her mother. So one day, when my grandmother came over, my mother sent me to my room to change my shirt, so I did, but I decided to do what Dad did. I put my shirt on inside out and backwards so the dirty spots didn't show. My grandmother immediately asked me, "Do you know you have your shirt inside out?" "Yes, I do," I replied. Of course, she wanted to know why. So I told her that that was what Dad did, so he could wear his shirt four times. I could see my mother in the kitchen listening and cracking up. My grandmother went right away to my mother to lecture her that she should not let me be like my father.

I couldn't help but think how some of the things we do as Christians might seem odd to others, but it is important that we be like our Heavenly Father.

> *"Blessed are they whose ways are blameless, who walk according to the law of the LORD. Blessed are they who keep his statutes and seek him with all their heart" (Ps. 119:1–2)*

My dad the hard working dairy farmer.

YOU CAN DO IT!

When we first got my dog Oreo, he was about one year old. We took him around the farm to get him used to it. I took him with me when I went to do chores. There were some steep steps around the barn that we'd trip on a lot. I took him up the steps and did my chores. When it came time to come back down, he wouldn't come—he was too scared. I went back up to him and told him, "You can do this," and then I went back down. He still just stood there and looked at me as if to say, *I can't do this*. I went back up to him again and told him, "You can do this!" and then I went back down again. I went back up to him the third time and said, "Oreo, I know you can do this!" Once more, I went down the steps, calling to him that he could do it.

And he did. In fact, he was so excited with his accomplishment that he ran up and down the stairs at least five times! He looked at me as if to say, *See, I did it!* Of course, now, years later, he goes up and down those stairs like there was never a problem.

It seems to me that God is often telling us that we can do something, encouraging us to do it. We think we can't do it. He says to us, "Yes, you can!" We need to have faith in Him, knowing that He has faith in us.

Philippians 4:13 tells us, "I can do all things through him (Christ) who gives me strength."

MY RADIO

When I was about fifteen years old, a neighbor girl had a radio that she didn't want anymore because she couldn't get her favorite stations on it because the antenna had broken off. She'd had it for about twelve years and didn't want to give it up, but wanted it at least to go to someone who would appreciate it. I told her I would like it and would use it in the barn when I was working. It was a digital radio, but it was so well used it was hard to read what station was on. Even though they were a bit static, it got all the stations that I liked—K-Love, Hope, and some country stations. My brother Frank would take it to the shop so he could listen to it, but it couldn't get his favorite stations, and he would get frustrated with it because it was hard to turn on. Actually, the first time he used it, he got so frustrated that he put it in the garbage, and I had to save it. He would borrow it again and the same thing would happen. This went on for years. My father would get frustrated with it too and call it junk. But I had it for about ten years until the cord got frayed, and I had to give up using it.

I was thinking—some people might think that you are useless and have nothing to offer. But God sees that there are useful things that you can do. He can use you in ways that will bring Him glory and honor. God will not give up on you.

WORKING FOR DAD

When it was time to work for Dad, it was a big responsibility. When we got old enough that Dad asked us to help him on the farm, we knew we could handle it. My two brothers and I waited for that time when he would be ready for our help and would call us. That would mean that we were mature enough to be of help to him. It was exciting for each of us. My brother Frank was the oldest and got called first. Then brother Jason was next. When was my turn going to be? I looked forward to being able to help Dad on the farm and leave the things I used to do behind and be with him outside. I was so excited when my turn finally came to be called to help my father. I was patient enough and finally it was my turn! Sometimes, we need to be patient and wait for God to call us and tell us what He wants us to do. We need to be mature enough and understand that we need to be patient. Because if we are not patient enough, we might get ourselves into a situation we cannot handle. We need to be patient and wait for God to call our name and give us our assignment. Then it will be wonderful, because He knows we are ready.

> *"Be patient, then brothers, until the Lord's coming. See how the farmer waits for the land to yield its valuable crop and how patient he is for the autumn and spring rains. You too, be patient and stand firm, because the Lord's coming is near" (James 5:7–8, NIV).*

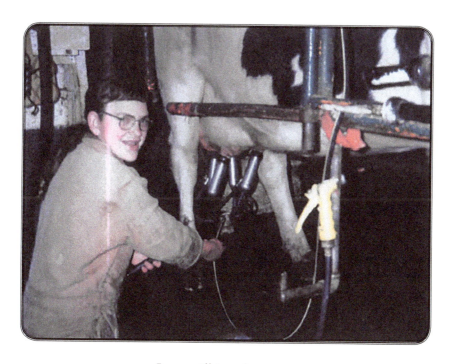

I am milking the cows.

MY CAT

I had to wait a long time to get a cat. I couldn't understand why, but God had a lesson for me. I would like to be married, but is it God's will for me to marry?

When I did finally get a cat, I realized that it is a responsibility. I understood why I had to wait for so long—I wasn't ready. Then later, when that cat had kittens, there was even more responsibility. It was a joy, but it was definitely a lot of work.

God lets us wait sometimes so we appreciate what He gives us more and also so we are better able to deal with the responsibility that comes with the gift.

So, I realized that I need to be patient about marriage. I will be more appreciative and ready for the responsibility when God does give it to me.

One of the fruits of the Spirit is patience: *"But the fruit of the Spirit is love, joy, peace, patience, kindness, goodness, faithfulness, gentleness and self-control" (Gal. 5:22).*

Juno and her nine kittens.

BEING WATCHED

My dog Oreo knows he is not supposed to go onto the road that goes in front of our farm. But sometimes, something must smell real good and he ventures onto or across the road. If we catch him, he knows he will be in trouble. Last night, he gave in to the temptation and went onto the road. But I saw him. I called him back, and obediently, he returned to me. Then we went into the house. A few minutes later, he kept whining, wanting to go out. So I let him out but went with him to make sure he didn't go back onto the road. Outside, he just looked at me. I said, "Go ahead, do what you want to do." And he just looked at me. He sat down and didn't move. We just stood there for a couple of minutes, looking at each other. Finally, I went back in the house, and he followed me and laid down on his bed. He didn't like it that I wouldn't let him do what he wanted to. While I was watching him, he wouldn't do it.

If we knew God was watching our every move, how many things that we wanted to do would we not do? If God were watching us right now, would He be happy about what we are doing?

> *"Set a guard over my mouth, O Lord; keep watch over the door of my lips. Let not my heart be drawn to what is evil, to take part in wicked deeds"* (Ps. 141:3, NIV).

My dog Oreo sitting on our wall.

CLEAN

When I was little, after playing all day and doing chores on the farm, my mom would tell me and my brothers to go get cleaned up. We would look at her and say, "What's the point? We're just going to go and get dirty again!" She would answer, "But it feels so good to be clean. It's a wonderful feeling." We didn't understand that really, until we got older. Gradually, we learned to clean up when we got dirty and try to look a little nicer. We knew what it felt like to be clean and acceptable to people that came over.

We are dirty in our sins, until God cleans us up, by saving us from our sins. When we accept Him as our Savior, we know what clean really feels like! This is why we need to stay clean. Whenever we begin to get dirty, we can go to God and ask forgiveness and get clean again.

> *"Come now, let us reason together, says the Lord. Though your sins be like scarlet, they shall be as white as snow; though they be red like crimson, they shall be as wool" (Isa. 1:18).*

I just got done with one of the dirty jobs on the farm.

COWS' CHRISTMAS

When I would have to work on Christmas Day, to help me remember the meaning of Christmas, I would tell the cows the Christmas story while I was feeding them. Each time I would tell the story, it might come out a little different. The cows didn't seem to mind the variations in the story, or even remember it from one year to the next! But what I would tell them would go something like this:

Once upon a time, a long time ago, Jesus, the Son of God, was born as a human baby. Because His family was traveling and there was no room in the hotel in the town of Bethlehem, they had to stay in a stable—maybe a little like the one we are in right now. His mother Mary and her husband Joseph knew He was a very special little baby and would grow up to be the Messiah, the Savior of the world. There were shepherds out in the fields who knew it too and came to worship Him. And then there were wise men who saw the star that appeared when He was born and came from the east also to worship Him and bring Him gifts. ("Come, Bossie, I'm telling a story. Get over here!") Now listen to the rest of the story. This Jesus grew up to be a man who was perfect, who never sinned, because He was God's Son. He chose twelve men to be his disciples to follow Him and learn from Him. They traveled all over Palestine, preaching the Gospel and healing the sick. But Jesus really came to be crucified later—to die—for all our sins (he took our penalty) so we could go to be with God when we die. But we have to believe that in our hearts. I bet you cows believe this story. It's true. It's in the Bible. But the best part is that this little baby who came, who grew up to die for us, also rose again from the dead and is now in heaven waiting for us. So, that's what happened long ago on this day. This is why I don't mind feeding you gals on Christmas—I get to tell you the story again.

Cows eating their hay in one of their many feeders.

MY TREE

When I was about ten, my brother and I went up the road a ways to visit my grandmother. She was working in her flower garden. Every spring, there were things that would pop up in her garden that she didn't want in there, including tree starts. She was about to pull some out, and we asked if we could have some tree starts. So she said we could each have one. So we took them home and planted them. I chose a certain spot by the road and planted mine there. My brother planted his but was not happy with the location and ended up moving it three or four times. It did not survive all the transplants, but mine grew tall and beautiful—so tall, in fact, that it started to reach up to the power lines. I didn't want it to get cut down or get its top cut off, so I prayed that my tree wouldn't get cut down. That winter, we had the worst snowstorm I can remember, and the weight of the snow actually bent the tree to the side so it was no longer a threat to the power lines. And now it is also a shade tree for the cattle and an "itching post" for them. All the lower limbs and trunk are rubbed smooth by the cows. It is still a beautiful tree.

Like the tree, we are sometimes bent by bad circumstances, but even then, we can be used by God to serve Him in special ways. We just need to "grow where we are planted" by God. We also need to realize that sometimes He might be "bending" us to keep us from getting into trouble.

> *"Consider it pure joy, my brothers, whenever you face trials of many kinds, because you know that the testing of your faith develops perseverance. Perseverance must finish its work so that you may be mature and complete, not lacking anything" (James 1:24).*

The tree before it got bent by a snowstorm.

WILD ONIONS

When I was a little girl, I was helping weed in the garden with my grandmother one day when we came upon a wild onion. I told her it smelled so good, but she said it was a weed and we needed to pull it. I asked her how she kept her garden looking so nice. She said a lot of it was hard work, but also talking to and taking care of the plants.

I got it into my head that by talking positively to the plants, it would help them grow beautifully, but talking negatively to them would make them die. So while walking home one day, I decided to try my theory out. I chose one plant by the roadside and talked positively to it. Then I went a little farther and talked negatively to a different plant. I did this for about a week, talking to the same plants.

It seemed to be working—the plant I talked positively to was looking good while the one I talked negatively to looked wilted.

As I got older, I discovered it is the same with animals. A friend came over who had two dogs. She was a very positive person, and her dogs reflected that attitude. Another person was very negative with her dog. You could see the difference between those dogs. The two "positive" dogs would greet the "negative" dog and get rejected, as if he was saying, *Leave me alone*, and then go to another room to get away from the two positive dogs.

It is the same way with kids. If there is a negative feeling in the home, the kids will reflect that attitude. Your kids and animals will show how things really are at home by their attitudes. What we show at home is who we actually are. So we need to be careful to be positive at home, so our kids will reflect that. I got all that from a wild onion!

"As a man thinks within himself, so he is" (Prov. 23:7, NASB).

BLACKBERRIES

In late summer, when the rest of the workers went out into the fields to bring in food for the cattle for winter, my brother and I wanted to help, but we were told we were too young. So we tried to think of things for the family that we could do. We decided to help by picking blackberries. We took two large stainless steel bowls across the road to the wild blackberry patch. We picked until both bowls were full. Then we found out they were so heavy that we couldn't carry them by ourselves. We had to each take a side and carry them together home one at a time. Mom was happy to get so many blackberries that she could use for jam and pies. And we were happy that we had been able to do something nice and useful for the family. That became our summer job—to pick the blackberries.

Sometimes, younger Christians may feel like they can't do as much as others in the body of Christ. They are still learning the ways of God and aren't qualified to serve in all areas until they have more experience and understanding. Yet there are always areas where even new believers can serve and we need to allow them to do what they can so they feel a part of the "family".

"Serve one another in love" (Gal. 5:13).

BLUE

On one of my parents' trips to the coast, they stopped in Florence. They went down to the docks where the fishing boats tie up. Fishing was slow, and one of the boats had puppies for sale. My parents looked at all fourteen and saw one they liked. They bought two toys for her to play with—a fish (because she came off a fishing boat) and a cow (because she was going to live on a dairy farm). The cow toy was almost as big as she was, seven inches long. The puppy was a blue Chihuahua so we named her "Blue". She was so small I was afraid my dad would step on her with his big feet. Around that time, my cat had kittens about the same size, and she accepted the puppy as part of her cat family. She loved to play with the kittens. She also loved anything with a motor, so I was afraid she would get run over by some of the farm equipment.

She has been worth all the work she was to care for. She was great company for us all these years. She is elderly now and has "accidents," but she is still part of our family, and we love her.

I am so glad that God continues to love us, even when we (like dogs) disobey, get underfoot, chase after things we shouldn't, and have "accidents." His love is unchanging.

My dad bring home a pizza in a box with
our dog blue sitting on the box.

BROTHERS

When I was about ten years old, my brother Jason noticed that I was having a difficult day. He said, "Tania, I know you are different in some ways. I know you are not like other kids, but I want to let you know that you are special in so many different ways. So just remember that when you are going through one of these hard days, thinking you don't understand things. Because you understand more things than most people. Just know that you are special." Remembering those words has brought me through a lot.

Even my older brother Frank has said good things to me when I was probably in my teenage years. I remember saying once, "I can't do this because…" "Stop right there," he said. "Do not say that you can't do something just because of your disabilities. I have a couple of disabilities myself! I don't use my disabilities as an excuse. If you can't do something, okay, just say so, but don't use your disability as an excuse, 'cause that's not right."

That got me thinking about how God often sends us someone to encourage us in some way. Usually, brothers pick on you. They tease you. They knock you around a little bit. You wouldn't think that God would use brothers to encourage you—in the end, they will be there if you really need them. Because you least expect it of them, it is extra special when they do step forward to defend you or protect you.

God loves us, and we are special in His eyes.

My two brothers and I in a cave.

WIDE OPEN

One time, when my brother and his girlfriend were preparing to go on a camping trip with my dad, some of their friends came over. So I took them out to where my brother was. I saw that the gate was wide open, which meant the cows could get out. I told my brother that the cows were in that pasture. He said, "Okay." Not sure if Frank was going to close it or not, I decided to do it myself. While I was doing it, Frank came up and said that he had opened it because he needed to back the truck and trailer into that yard. But he went off somewhere else, so eventually I shut the gate myself, knowing he could open it again if he needed to.

When I got back to the house, my older brother was having a party with some of his friends. So, not wanting to hang around with them, I went upstairs to my room where I stayed the rest of the night. But I did pray before I went to bed that the cows wouldn't get out.

The next morning, my dad and I both got up early, since they were leaving soon on their camping trip. When we got out to the trailer of hay, we saw the gate was wide open! Since taking care of the animals is pretty much my responsibility, I felt I should have made sure the gate was shut. I told my dad that even though I hadn't checked the gate before I went to bed, I did something even better. "What's that?" he said. "I prayed that the cows wouldn't get out, and that's even better than shutting the gate." "Well, yes," he said. Then my brother came out and admitted that he hadn't shut the gate and was relieved that the cows hadn't gotten out.

You might not be in a right relationship with God. That leaves you "wide open" for attack. You might think you are okay and not in any danger. But you don't know how many people may be praying for you to keep you from danger—your mother, grandmother, aunt or uncle or siblings. Although you may be wide open to attack right now, it is their prayers that may be keeping you from trouble.

GOING NOWHERE

I was on a track team when I was a senior in high school. I spent much time running around and around the track. I kept thinking how much fun it would be to be actually running somewhere rather than just running around the track going nowhere! One day, my coach decided that I could run on the road. Finally, I thought, I can go somewhere. He gave me so many minutes for this run. I went running in a direction I had never gone before and came to a bend. It scared me—could I find my way back? How long would it take me to return? So I decided to turn around and run back. I went to my coach who asked me if I had run all the minutes he told me to run. I told him that I hadn't. I told him, "I kinda got scared. I had never run that far before, and I didn't know how long it would take to get back." He told me that I needed to run four more laps around the track because I hadn't obeyed him. So I did and here I was, going nowhere again—in circles! I should have obeyed him.

So often, it's that way with God. He gives us an assignment, but we get scared or think we know better. When He asks us about what we did, we have to admit that we didn't complete the task and then we find ourselves going around in circles again. God will let us go nowhere for a while until He sees that we are ready to try again.

This is very much like the story of Jonah, who ran away instead of obeying God and going to preach to Ninevah. He ended up spending three miserable days inside the belly of a fish before he decided it would be better to obey God. God gave him another chance and told him to go preach to Ninevah. This time, he went and preached, and the entire city repented. Now Jonah was going somewhere! (Book of Jonah)

I TOLD YOU SO!

One of the jobs we kids had to do on the farm was to feed baby calves. That could be a pretty big job. We had to take so many bottles' worth of powdered milk (mixed with water in a bucket) that we needed for the calves. Then we would have to carry that to the calf barn quite a distance away and then feed the calves. We did this every morning and every night. But then our friends would come over and want to play. We'd tell them we had chores to do before we could play. Sometimes, they'd come with us and offer to help so it would go faster. I'd tell them not try to carry a bucket that was too heavy and to be sure and stay only on the stepping stones going to the barn. They'd mumble a bit and ask why. I'd tell them, but sometimes they'd take the quicker way and step off the stones. They'd slip or sink into the muck, spill the milk, and get all muddy. Of course, I'd say, "I told you so!" They would not be very happy about that, or about having to go back and get more milk. When we'd get to the barn, I'd tell them I'd turn the light on, and they should duck when they walk in. "Why?" they'd ask. "You'll see," I'd say and reach in and turn the light on. Bats would fly out. They soon saw why it was a good idea to duck! They didn't want to hear "I told you so" again! They didn't want to admit that we knew a lot. But we did these chores day in and day out and had learned some things.

Sometimes, we don't want to listen to our elders, even though they have had experience and know more than we do. But for our own good, we need to respect their knowledge and advice. It's no fun to hear "I told you so!"

"Pay attention and listen to the sayings of the wise;
apply your heart to what I teach" (Prov. 22:17).

AM / FM

When my dad was working out in the garden one day, he turned on the radio, but he could not get his favorite stations. He could only get static, or some different language program. He couldn't understand what happened to his regular stations. He was getting frustrated, until he thought to check what frequency he was on. He had it on AM instead of FM!

I was thinking that maybe that is what we do sometimes. We try to listen to God, but it seems we only get static or things we don't understand. Maybe, if we get on the same wavelength as God, we would understand a lot more. We can get on the same frequency as God by reading His Word, and when we are on the same wavelength as God, we will understand what He is telling us. His Word, the Bible, is what we must tune in to.

The apostle Paul says in his letter to the church in Colossi, *"We have not stopped praying for you and asking God to fill you with the knowledge of his will; through all spiritual wisdom and understanding. And we pry this in order that you may live a life worthy of the Lord and may please Him in every way, bearing fruit in every good work, growing in the knowledge of God" (Col. 1:9–10).*

TRUST ME

I went to the feed store when I was about ten years old with my dad and brothers. Sometimes at the feed store, there are animals that are being given away by someone who can't keep them anymore. On this particular day, there was a guinea pig being given away. "I guess you can have a guinea pig," Dad said, "since your mom is away on vacation."

When we got home, Jason and I were playing with the guinea pig in my room. I had the cat in my lap. Jason said, "Let the cat go." And I said, "Why should I do that? The cat would probably go right after the guinea pig!" "Oh no," Jason said, "Trust me, we're right here. He wouldn't do it."

I gave in and let the cat go. Guess what? The cat went straight for the guinea pig, sniffed it, grabbed it by the neck and left the room! Jason took out after them, got the guinea pig out of the cat's mouth, and put the cat outside. The guinea pig survived about three days until Mom got back from her trip.

Another similar memory was of a baby goat. I chased it down to catch and show it to some friends of my brother. It was pretty wild, but I was able to catch it. It kept trying to get away, but Jason said, "Trust me, it's okay. Let it go!" I remembered the cat and the guinea pig, though, and said no. I knew it would just run away.

Because of experiences like these, when we learn not to trust people, it is sometimes hard for us to trust God. Because God knows our entire circumstances, when He says, "Trust Me," we can!

"Trust in the Lord with all your heart, and lean not on your own understanding; in all your ways acknowledge Him and He will make your paths straight" (Prov. 3:5).

Some of our baby goats.

THE RIGHT LABEL

One time, when I was helping my dad set out plants in the garden, transferring them from the pots into the dirt, Dad would hand me the label for the plant. I was thinking that if I accidentally put the wrong label on the plant, we would be expecting that plant to do something that it wasn't able to do. The right label, however, would tell us what it was expected to do.

We too need to be sure that we have the right label on us. We should not try to do something that we are not labeled to do. If God has labeled us His children, then we are expected to act like His children. If people look at our label and we are producing "different fruit" than expected, we are not making God look good. We need to follow what our label says.

> *"This is how we know who are the children of God and who the children of the devil are: Anyone who does not do what is right isn't a child of God; nor is anyone who does not love his brother." (1 John 3:10, NIV).*

> *The Bible also tells us that it is by our fruit that we can be recognized (Matt. 7:20).*

HUG ME

When I was little, I had a teddy bear that had a shirt that had "Hug Me" on it. Of all my stuffed animals, that teddy bear was my favorite. That was the one I considered my best friend and the one I chose to go everywhere with me. Somewhere, I lost that bear, but I still remember him like he was when I was young. I remember him like he was when he was brand-new. But when I really think about it, I remember that he had his nose about to fall off; the "Hug Me" was almost worn off the shirt; there were places where the fur was gone.

When something or someone is special to you, like that teddy bear was to me, you don't notice the bad things. You just remember the good things. I think that is how it is with love. If there is a special person we love, as time goes by, we don't see the aging process. We remember them like they were when we first met them. I look forward to the day when I have a husband and will be able to see him that way.

God created man and woman as perfect beings. Like Tania and the teddy bear, He wanted a special relationship with the people He had made. He wanted to be with them for eternity. But man chose to disobey God and then had to suffer the consequences of sin. Yet, even though man wore (and we wear today) the bad consequences of sin, God still provided a way to restore that relationship through His Son Jesus Christ.

> *"Therefore, if anyone is in Christ, he is a new creation; the old has gone; the new has come! All this is from God, who reconciled us to Himself through Christ" (2 Cor. 5:17–18).*

BEAUTIFUL

My dog Cocoa was part miniature husky. He had a lot of fur and would get hot in the summer. I decided one summer that I would cut his hair so he would be more comfortable. My mom didn't know if I should. I was only eight at the time, but she was so busy that she let me do it.

That poor dog when I got done with him, he was so ashamed. That day, when someone came to visit, Cocoa did not meet them like he usually did. I went looking for him and found him under my bed. He wouldn't come out when I called him, and when he finally did come out, he was a very unhappy dog. He just kept his head down the whole time, so ashamed of how he looked.

I got to thinking that sometimes we are ashamed of ourselves—of what we look like. My mom would remind me that the same God that made poodles made bulldogs! (God does have a sense of humor.)

We didn't like Cocoa any less because his fur was cut. The whole point is that it is not what we look like that is important, but who we are as a person. You may be ugly on the outside, but beautiful on the inside, or beautiful on the outside but ugly inside. We need to develop those qualities of character that make us beautiful inside (love, joy, peace, patience, etc.).

> Because "the Lord does not look at the things man looks at. Man looks at the outward appearance, but the Lord looks at the heart" (1 Sam. 16:7, NIV).

My dog Cocoa.

COCOA

I was about three years old when we got Cocoa, a miniature husky. He was a good dog. When he got older, he treated us like we were his puppies! He was always watching out for us.

When I was about sixteen, I got asked out to a homecoming dance. I had never gone to something like that. I didn't even know how to dance. The boy who asked me said that he would come over with his sister and show me some steps. Cocoa did not like it at all that I was dancing with a boy.

He jumped on us and barked furiously, trying to separate us. When the boy stepped away, Cocoa put his paw on my legs and wanted me to dance with him! He did not like this boy "cutting in" to dance with me! He kept jumping on us whenever the boy tried to show me some more steps. In his mind, Cocoa was protecting me from this boy he did not trust. He was afraid I would get hurt. He wanted this boy to know that I belonged to him.

When we accept Jesus as our Savior, we belong to God and He is a jealous God, wanting us to worship Him and no other (like Cocoa was with me). In Exodus 20, God says that we should worship no other because He is a "jealous God."

Our Puppy Cocoa and I playing.

MY DUCKS

One day, my dad called and told me to get the incubator ready because a friend had found a nest of eggs abandoned, because the mother duck had been killed. Three weeks passed and eleven little ducklings hatched! For a week, I kept them in the sewing room where I could keep an eye on them. Then I moved them into the basement. They needed a pool so I prayed that God would give me ideas. He did! I used a dog carrier, put water in it, tipped it, and this way, the little ducks could walk in and out of it and use it like a pool. I found a wading pool to use when they got a little bigger. But I was concerned how they would manage when it got time to put them out in the pond. Being a "mother duck" was new to me, and I prayed that God would take care of these little ducklings. I placed them in the pond, and when I went out to give them some feed, I saw a mother and father goose with little goslings that had "adopted" the ducklings. It gave me a warm feeling in my heart to see that God had cared for the little ducklings by giving them a "family" that could show them how to live in the wild.

The world can be a scary place for us too. We need to remember that God is there to help us; to send people into our lives to show us the way and help us.

God promises us this kind of help in Philippians 4:19: "My God will meet all your needs according to His glorious riches in Christ Jesus."

My 11 ducks swimming in the pond.

GIVEN A CHANCE

My dad has a garden that he works very hard on every year. When the planting season is over, there are often leftover plants in the stores. They are the ones that have been picked over, damaged or wilting and are about to be thrown away. In a last chance to make a little money, the stores will mark them down in price. That's when my dad goes in and buys them. He gives them another chance. Even though they were passed over, they still have something to give. I've seen many plants that looked pretty sad, actually do very well with my dad's nurturing.

People are like that. Sometimes, they just need to be given another chance to show how productive and beautiful they can be. Giving a "reject" a chance is the most important thing you can do for them. Only then can we know what wonderful things they are capable of.

I am reminded of the story in the Bible called the Good Samaritan. This was the third person that passed by a man lying beside the road, beaten and wounded. He was a Samaritan (a race despised by the Jews), but he took pity on the man and took him to an inn and paid for his care. He gave this man a second chance (Luke 10).

ORANGE WAGON

When my brother Jason and I were little, we had this orange wagon that we would pull everywhere. One day, we decided to see if my dad had anything he needed hauled. He was pretty far out in a distant field. So we tugged the wagon way out there and asked, "Dad, do you need any help?" You could tell he was thinking, *They came all the way out here to offer me help?* He thought a minute and then said, "There are some crabapples over there. Why don't you fill the wagon with them?" So we went over and started picking up crabapples off the ground and putting them in our wagon. We tired of that pretty fast and started for home.

The field we had to go through to get home was pretty rough with a lot of ruts. Before long, we only had a couple dozen apples left in the wagon, and we were getting tired. As we went on, we told a story that my grandmother told my dad, and he told the story to us when we got tired. About two frogs that jumped into a cream can and couldn't get out. They kept swimming and swimming until one finally tired and sank to the bottom. The other frog kept on swimming until he too got too tired and started floating and then he jumped out. (The cream had turned to butter.) We told the story to encourage one another to keep going. We did get back to the house with probably only a dozen of the apples but telling the story helped us keep going.

I got to thinking that it is a lot about Bible stories that encourage us to keep on going and not give up. God told Joshua to be courageous. He told Moses He would help him. God is always there. The apostle Paul told the Galatian church, *"Let us not become weary in doing good, for at the proper time we will reap a harvest if we do not give up. Therefore, as we have opportunity, let us do good to all people, especially to those who belong to the family of believers"* (Gal. 6:9–10).

THE ROUND BARN

Sometimes, my brother frustrates me. Like when he stack the firewood in the middle of the barn, right in the path I use to do my chores in the barn! Firewood is dangerous and just clutter when it is in the wrong place. I couldn't help but think how like us that is.

We must be careful not to clutter up our lives. Sin and guilt clutter our lives and block the work of the Holy Spirit. Just as we need to keep the path safe and clear in the barn, we need to keep our lives clear of sin.

This concept of sin entangling us is explained in Hebrews 12:1:

> *"Therefore since we are surrounded by such a great cloud of witnesses, let us throw of everything that hinders and the sin that so easily entangles, and let us run with perseverance the race marked out for us."*

The round barn and some of our Holstein calves.

TWO DOGS AND A CAT

I have two dogs and a cat that chase each other all over the house, romping, jumping, and being rowdy. But when I sit down in the chair and they come to me, they know they must be quiet and calm. All three will climb onto my lap and settle down. I look at them—they are curled up, touching each other, content.

I think church is like that. God is our thing in common. When we come to church, we need to be at peace with one another and worship God!

"Get rid of all bitterness, rage and anger, brawling and slander, along with every form of malice. Be kind and compassionate to one another, forgiving each other, just as in Christ forgave you.." (Eph. 4:31–32).

> *"May the God who gives endurance and encourage-ment give you a spirit of unity among yourselves as you follow Christ Jesus, so that with one heart and mouth you may glorify the God and Father of our Lord Jesus Christ" (Rom. 15:5).*

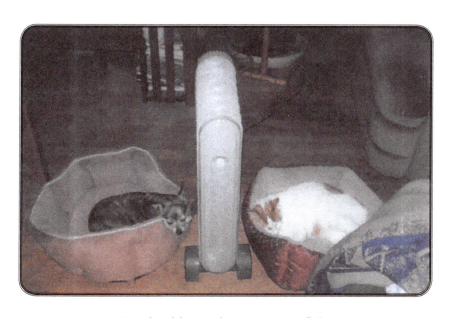

Our dog blue and our cat snowflake.

COACH

Having a good coach is important. He can teach you things about life. I remember when I played on the volleyball team, the older girls played on the first string, and we were on the second string. I especially remember one game we played. Our team was doing really well. The A team girls were boasting about how well they were playing, how good they were, how bad the other team was and even ran down the coach. My coach got tired of hearing what they were saying. He called a time-out and brought all the first string girls in and told them to sit down. "Why?" they complained. He said, "You do not have respect for the other team, and you don't have respect for me, so you do not deserve to play."

And coach had us on the second string to go onto the court to play, and we weren't even yet into the second half of the game. We were surprised, but we went. We respected our coach and the other team, but we weren't very good volleyball players. This tortured the first string to watch us start to lose the game for our side. They begged the coach to let them back in to the game. He said, "Do you understand why I took you out?" "Yes," they replied. "We will try to be better." So coach let them back into the game, and they proceeded to play well and win the game for us.

God is like a coach. If we do things that do not please God or have a bad attitude, He will "take us out" until we learn to have more respect. Others may have to step up to do the job who are not as well qualified, but their attitude pleases Him better.

"A man's pride brings him low, but a man of lowly spirit gains honor" (Prov. 29:23, NIV).

74

OREO COOKIES

Every Wednesday, when we were little, my brothers and I would go down to the woods and sit on a log and eat Oreo cookies. One Wednesday, it was pouring down rain, so we chose to eat our cookies in an old pickup that was sitting out in the woods. My brother Frank found out one of the walkie-talkies that he let Jason played with its back was missing. So Frank told Jason that we couldn't return until the back was found. Jason whispered and asked me if I knew how to get home? I was about six at the time, but I assured him that I thought so. So, we got the door open on the pickup and started running. When I got to the gate, I looked back and saw that Frank had caught Jason, who squirmed away. Then I saw Frank pick up something off the ground, which turned out to be the missing walkie-talkie back. It was pouring rain, but we all made it to the house where Mom met us and told us to get our wet clothes off and come have supper.

I was thinking that sometimes there are things in our past that keep us from going forward. But if we have accepted Jesus Christ as our Savior, we can always "go home" where He is waiting for us, ready to help us get through anything.

> *John 14:23 says, "Jesus replied, if anyone loves me, he will obey my teaching. My Father will love him, and we will come to him and make our home with him."*

POTATOES IN THE GARDEN

Late in the season one year, Dad told me to go dig up the potatoes in the garden. It was past the harvesttime, and I didn't think there were any more potatoes. In fact, I looked at the garden and didn't see any sign of anything growing there. But he said, "Go, dig."

So I got the shovel and went and started digging in the ground. To my amazement, I found about twenty potatoes! I went to my father and said, "How did you know I would find anything there?" He just replied that he knew what he had planted there and knew they would be there.

I was thinking that is how God is. He "plants" things in people, and He knows when it is time to harvest them. So when He tells us to go help someone, even if we don't see why, He knows what we don't. But when you listen to God and do what He says, you will see why He sent you.

> *"Let us not become weary in doing good, for at the proper time we will reap a harvest if we do not give up"* (Gal. 6:9).

Dad holding our dog and a giant beet we grew in the garden.

TREE HOUSE

My brother Jason and I decided we would like to paint the wood tree house that Dad had built for us. We were trying to figure out what colors to paint it. Should we do it barn red? Or black and white zebra striped? We wanted it to match the décor of the farm. I came up with the idea of painting it like a Holstein cow, since we were a dairy farm. Jason thought a few minutes and then said, "I've got an idea. Why don't we paint it like a Holstein cow?" "But," I said, "I just said that a few minutes ago!" He insisted it was his original idea. I gave in and said, "Whatever."

In other situations, we might come up with an idea and like Jason, others might think it was their idea. I say so what? If it is a good idea and does good, then be happy that it is working, no matter who gets the credit for it. The important thing is that it works and something special comes out of it. All the credit should go to God anyway, since He is the giver of all good ideas. We shouldn't always want the praise for ourselves. Even if someone takes the praise away from us, we know who really deserves the praise!

"Through Jesus, therefore, let us continually offer to God a sacrifice of praise—the fruit of lips that confess His name. And do not forget to do good and to share with others, for with such sacrifices God is pleased" (Heb. 13:15).

Our tree house on the farm.

IN THE WATER

Our whole family was swimming in the pond one summer day along with our two dogs—Cocoa, a miniature husky (who liked to swim), and Kojak, the other dog who didn't. The dogs took off after something, which we saw later was a raccoon. The raccoon jumped into the water to try to get away from the dogs. Cocoa jumped in after it, while the other dog stayed on land, watching. But when Cocoa got near the raccoon, the raccoon tried to hold Cocoa's head under the water. Dad saw this and realized that the raccoon was trying to kill Cocoa by drowning. He swam out to save Cocoa. The raccoon would not let go of Cocoa, so Dad drug Cocoa to land with the raccoon hanging on all the way! Once on land, the raccoon let go and took off with both dogs in pursuit.

But what hit me was that there are those people who try to "pull us under" and keep us in "deep water". They would rather see us addicted to things that are sinful, like they are. We have to trust in God (like my dad) to pull us to safety and free us from these bad things that like to hang on to us.

We are reminded of that in Psalm 46:1, *"God is our refuge and strength, an ever-present help in trouble."*

Our pond on the farm.

CACTUS

I got hurt at least a hundred times by the cactus we have in our house! I finally went to Dad to ask why we have a cactus. A cactus plant is painful! Dad said to wait, that the cactus will bloom some day and it would be the most beautiful thing to see. He said that it would be worth all the pain of taking care of it and running into it!

It did bloom eventually and was truly beautiful. I think we must be a real pain to God sometimes—ugly and prickly and painful. He loves us enough to continue to care for us—to discipline and prune until we produce the blooms or fruit that He intends for us.

I am reminded of the story that Jesus told about the vinedresser and the vines. The vinedresser nurtures, lifts up, and even prunes the branches of the grapevines so that they will bear much fruit. The harvest makes all the work of tending the vines worthwhile, just as the bloom of the cactus made all the work of taking care of it worthwhile (John 15:1–17).

One of our cactuses that bloomed and two dogs. Aren't they cute?

THREE FISH

When Jason and I were younger, we used to spend time at the pond. Once, we found a bunch of little fish by the bank. We decided to try to catch one of each type of fish. We got our goldfish net and a container and proceeded to catch three fish. We took them home and put them in our old goldfish tank so we could watch them closely and study the differences in them. Then when they got too big for the tank, we put them in the cow trough. We'd feed them every day and check on them. One day, we noticed that when a cow would come to the trough to drink, the grain would wash off her nose into the water and the fish would eat it! This was good news for us because now we didn't have to feed the fish—they were getting their food from the cows!

I was thinking that we are like that. God chooses us to serve Him and puts us in a place where He can feed and nurture us and teach us what He wants us to learn. He may move us around to another place where He can teach us other things. But He always provides for our needs.

And wherever He places us, remember what this verse says: *"My God will meet all your needs according to His glorious riches in Christ Jesus" (Phil. 4:19).*

ASK ME

My dad and I were working on a fence that we really needed to get done before hay season. We wanted the cows to be able to be in this new pasture area with lots of grass. Dad told me that he would never ask me to do something that he hadn't done. And I remembered that other times, he would do something for a while to show me how to do it. He had theories about how something should be done, usually because he had tried them out. He would never ask us to do something that he hadn't done, and he already figured out the best way to do it. That's one of the reasons we were so willing to help him. Also we wanted to show our love to him for all the things he had done for us.

It is the same way with God. He came to this earth and did many of the same things we do. So when He asks me to do something for Him, I want to do it. And I know that with His help, I can do what He asks. I want to do it because I love Him. And I know He will be there for me.

> *"Whatever you do, work at it with all your heart, as working for the Lord, not for men, since you know that you will receive an inheritance from the Lord as a reward. It is the Lord Christ you are serving"* (Col. 3:23–24).

THE DUCK BLIND

My brother Jason and I would run all over the farm when we were little. One day, we found ourselves by a duck blind. Being curious, we decided to go check it out. We climbed into it with our dog Cocoa and proceeded to latch it from the inside. When we were ready to go home, we found out it was easier to latch it then to unlatch it! We couldn't unlatch it! I panicked. No one knew where we were. We'd never get out. We'd die in there of starvation! My brother tried to reassure me that I needed to relax—we'd figure a way to get out. If we don't, Dad would come looking for us, and he would find us. I tried to relax and have faith in Jason. He was working the whole time trying to figure out the latching. To my relief, he did manage to get it unlatched and we were able to get out.

It made me realize how often we get ourselves into situations that cause us to panic. We tend to worry and fret about the details. What we need to remember is our Heavenly Father and have faith in Him. There is a wonderful verse in Philippians that confirms this:

> *"Do not be anxious about anything, but in every-thing, by prayer and petition with thanksgiving, present your requests to God. And the peace of God, which transcends all understanding, will guard your hearts and your minds in Christ Jesus"* (Phil. 4:6–7).

THE GREENHOUSE

Dad and I decided to put together a do-it-yourself kit greenhouse. "Easy to assemble," the instructions said. It turned out that "easy to assemble" also meant "easy to disassemble." We'd put one piece together, only to have another pop apart. It seems like we put it all together at least five times! Finally, we got it together and it looked pretty good—like a greenhouse.

How many times are we frustrated with our lives that seem to be always popping out of place. We have to keep piecing back together parts of our lives. I couldn't help but think of how hard it must be for someone who gets out of prison to piece back together their life. Something that used to be easy is now hard, because of the choices that they made. We need to work at helping those who really need help piecing their lives back together. We can show them love and caring in practical ways.

The completed and functional greenhouse was our reward and so it can be with people. If they accept help and begin making better choices because of what we have done for them, we will all share in their reward.

> "In Him (Jesus) the whole building is joined together and rises to become a holy temple in the Lord. And in Him you too are being built together to become a dwelling in which God lives by His Spirit" (Eph. 2:21–22).

I DARE YOU!

When I was about nine years old, I was playing with my cousins at my uncle's place, I was telling them about my dad, how he used to go barefoot; he'd even do all his chores barefoot, which included getting the cows in for milking. On cold summer days, he'd deliberately step into fresh, steaming cow pies with each foot to keep his feet warm. My cousins said, after hearing the story, "I bet you wouldn't do anything like that." "Oh yes, I would!" I said. So they dared me to climb over the fence and put my feet in a fresh cow pie. "Okay," I said and took my shoes off, jumped over the fence, and stepped into a fresh cow pie. My uncle decided to take that moment to come check on us. He looked at me and then at my cousins. "You weren't thinking of doing that too, were you?" he asked them. "Oh no, we just wanted to see if Tania would do it, so we dared her."

"Well," he said to me, "Tania, I want you to jump back over the fence, go over the hose, and wash your feet off, then put your socks and shoes back on." So I did what he said, but I noticed him walking back to the house, smiling and shaking his head, probably going to tell my aunt what I just did. But she wouldn't be surprised—after all, my dad was her brother.

Sometimes, I think, God dares us to be like Him. He will not dare us to step into fresh cow pies, but He does "dare" us, by commanding us, *"I am the Lord your God; consecrate yourselves and be holy, because I am holy"* (Lev. 11:44).

This is a dare we all need to take!

THE FROG

When I was helping my dad with fencing one time, I looked into one of the postholes that was already dug. I saw something in there, so I reached in to see what it was—a frog! I try to grab the frog; it was too wet. I finally got it out, and Dad told me to go put it in the pond. As I was walking to the pond with this frog, I was thinking about the fairytale story where when the princess kissed the frog and he turned into a prince and they lived happily ever after.

I couldn't help but think how in real life we wish it were that simple. We wonder who we will marry. What will he be like? When will it happen? Yet we know that relationships, in reality, take time. The best thing to do is to pray and ask God to guide you. He has a plan for your life, and that includes the person you will marry.

"I know the plans I have for you, plans to give you hope and a future." This is what the Lord says in Jeremiah 29:11. Ever so much better and safer than kissing a frog!

A GOOD POST

My dad and I were fencing one day, and I was trying to help him put in a post. There was a certain way it had to be. It had to be straight. I'd look at it and say, "Does it really matter?" "Yes, it does," he'd answer. It needs to have a good foundation and be straight. If it is not put in right, it could fall over and compromise the whole fence. Then the animals could get out.

We too need to have a good foundation. We need to know what we believe in. We need to be linked with supportive friends and family. The foundation is our faith in Jesus Christ. We build on this foundation by studying God's Word.

"If you confess with your mouth Jesus as Lord, and believe in your heart that God raised Him from the dead, you shall be saved" (Rom. 10:9). This is how we become a believer in Jesus Christ. The next step in this building process is to know and study God's Word.

> *"Study to show yourself approved unto God, a workman that does not need to be ashamed, rightly dividing the word of truth" (2 Tim. 2:15).*

Some of our animals behind the fences.

POCKETS OF KNOWLEDGE

In the process of growing up, I learned a whole bunch of different jobs to do around the farm. Now that I am older, I don't have a "résumé" of things I have done to present to a person hiring me. Maybe I'm meant for something more.

Maybe I'm not meant to work for someone else. Maybe I'm meant to do more than that.

Maybe God has something special planned for me—something that will use all the different jobs I have done. Maybe God can use me even more than other people might think. Because they don't know what I can do. God has been my teacher and my mentor.

Maybe He has taught me specific things for His plan.

So, someday, when I do leave the farm, my pockets of knowledge will go with me. Through all the times of learning, of pain, of hardship, God has been teaching me and preparing me.

> *"I know the plans I have for you, declares the Lord, plans to prosper you and not to harm you, plans to give you hope and a future" (Jer. 29:11).*

DEEP WATER

I remember Mom would always tell us to be careful in our pond—
not to swim in the pond without some kind of flotation device; never
swim alone; and, of course, "be careful!"

It was a hot day and by the time I got into the pond, all the kids
who had been swimming with my brothers were gone. The only one
left was my brother Frank, sitting on the dock in the middle of the
pond. I decided to swim out to him, even though it was quite a ways.
I didn't have anything to float with, but I told myself at least I was
only breaking one of the rules. What I didn't know was that Frank
hadn't seen me. I had only gotten part way when I realized that I had
made a mistake. Reeds wrapped around my feet and started pulling
me under, and I felt like I was sinking. I wondered if I was going to
drown. Why hadn't I listened to my mother? Then I remembered
that Mom had told us if we get into a bad situation while swimming,
just to float on our backs. I did, and the reeds fell away, and I was able
to continue on and reach the dock. When I got to the dock, Frank
was surprised to see me, so he would not have been any help to me.

Remembering this story made me think that there are times in
life when we feel like we are drowning, being pulled under by circumstances. Often, it is because we haven't listened to God who has
given us instructions about things we shouldn't do. We think it won't
hurt, and we just go ahead and do it. And yet God is always there,
and He is ready to help us.

> "I seek You (God) with all my heart; do not let me
> stray from your commands. I have hidden Your
> Word in my heart that I might not sin against you"
> (Ps. 119:10–11, NIV).

RECOGNIZABLE

Dad, Mom, and I were returning from a trip one time, arriving at the airport. Dad had arranged with Frank, my oldest brother, to pick us up. He agreed to meet us at the baggage claim area. After we came down the escalators to the baggage claim area, we looked around but didn't see Frank. There was only a homeless-looking man sleeping on a bench in an old overcoat, with long hair and a beard. We claimed our luggage and still didn't see Frank anywhere. Dad called home and my other brother, Jason, said that Frank had left in plenty of time and should be at the airport. So we circled the area again and this time, the sleeping man by the escalators sat up and looked at us. It was Frank! We just hadn't recognized him.

It got me thinking about Christians. Are we recognizable? We need to act like God wants us to act—like Jesus. And if we don't act like Jesus, we look like everybody else. We don't look like His children. If we look like God's children, the unsaved will recognize us as someone they can come to for help. If they see that we are different, they can come up to us and ask us why we are. If we look like everybody else, they won't expect us to have any more answers than anyone else. We need to be recognizable as Christians. Because…

"If our gospel is hid, it is hid to them that are lost"
(2 Cor. 4:3, KJV).

ROLE MODEL

When I was in high school, I helped out a second grade teacher with her kids. After I graduated and when I was about twenty, I came back one time to go to a football game and saw several of my acquaintances whom I hung out with when I was at school. The reason I hung out with them is because I felt no one else wanted me around. One of them lit up a cigarette in front of me. I had the thought that what if one of the second graders whom I had helped with saw me with these kids who were smoking. What would they think of me? I decided that from then on, I would choose carefully the people I hung out with. If my friends could not respect me for who I was, then they didn't need to hang out with me. Nor me with them. I needed to hang out with people who were good for me—people that God could use for the good in my life. We need to ask ourselves, do we want to be like the people we hang out with, or do we want to be someone different? With better people around you, you will in turn be a better role model for others. And you can show your friends who God is and how important He is to you. And you can be a good role model.

> *"Do not be yoked together with unbelievers. For what do righteousness and wickedness have in common? Or what fellowship can light have with darkness?" (2 Cor. 6:14).*

> *"Let your light shine before men, that they may see your good deeds and praise your Father in heaven" (Matt. 6:14).*

EAT RIGHT

For a while, when I was in my twenties, I tried to eat more healthy. I avoided junk food and ate more vegetables to see if that would make me feel better. When I'd tell others, they always had their ideas of what I should be eating. I would have been more inclined to follow their suggestions if I had seen them eating the things they were telling me about. Often, the things they would tell me to do, they weren't doing themselves. Why should I do it when they weren't? I began to get a little irritated, because I thought I was eating pretty healthily on my own.

We need to be careful when telling others how to do things if we aren't doing them ourselves. We need to walk our talk. We'll be a lot better off if we show them, not just tell them. The most important thing we can show them is how to live for God. This came to me while I was out in the field working in the hay with Dad. A similar thought came to James, the author of the epistle. He said, *"Do not merely listen to the word, and so deceive yourselves. Do what it says"* (James 1:22).

SAYING THANK YOU

As children, we had many chores to do around the farm. We were kept busy on the farm and didn't go many places or have many visitors. I was afraid we would forget how to be polite to people. So I decided that to keep in practice, I was going to be polite to all the animals I took care of by saying "thank you," "please," and "excuse me" to them. By being polite to God's animals, I was reminded that I needed to be respectful and grateful to God, too.

Being thankful to God should be something automatic and effortless to us. We should get up in the morning saying, "Thank you, Lord, for this day," and go to bed at night saying, "Thank you, Lord, for the day we've had." He has given us so much that being thankful should always be in our thoughts.

When we are reminded to be polite to others, let's not forget to be thankful to God.

> *"Be joyful always; pray continually, give thanks in all circumstances, for this is God's will for you in Christ Jesus" (1 Thess. 5:18).*

AIRPLANE

When I was about sixteen years old, my mom and I went to Montana to visit my mother's brother who was a pastor. Sometimes, he would take us up in his plane. This time, he let me sit right next to him (in the copilot's seat). And when we got up in the air, he asked me if I wanted to take the stick and fly. I said, "No, thank you." And sat on my hands! I did not trust myself to fly a plane. I was thinking that if I put my hand on the stick, the plane might go down because I was trying to fly it. But he was a good pilot and was right there. He would not have let anything like that happen.

Sometimes, when God asks us to do something, we are afraid that if we try it, something might go wrong. We need to remember that God doesn't ask us to do anything we are incapable of, and He will enable us to do it.

> God says, "I will instruct you and teach you in the way you should go; I will counsel you and watch over you" (Ps. 32:8, NIV).

My uncle getting ready to take my mother,
and brothers and I up in the plane.

FOOTPRINTS

When I was young, my brothers and I would help my dad out in the cornfield. Sometimes, as we walked down the rows, it would be muddy, and we'd watch the footprints my father made with his big boots. We'd try to step in his footprints and walk like he walked, but he was six feet tall and had fourteen-inch long feet. Our legs were too short, and we just couldn't do it. But as we grew older, we kept trying. We were so happy when we finally got big enough that we could walk in his footsteps.

I remember one time when we went to the beach, I saw lots of footprints in the sand. I thought it was great fun to try to walk in those footprints too. There were so many different prints representing so many different types of people and different ways of walking. It was always difficult, because these were not my own footprints.

We need to remember that we need to not follow the path of others, but to follow the path of our Father in heaven. God shows us His path through His Word.

"Your Word is a lamp to my feet and a light to my path" (Ps. 119:105).

"Our goal would be able to say with the psalmist: *"My steps have held to your paths; my feet have not slipped" (Ps. 17:5).*

THE BIRD

When spring comes, we start working on things around the farm that need to be fixed—things we couldn't do because of the cold in the winter. One day, when I was out working on something, my dog Oreo was with me. He unintentionally walked next to a killdeer bird nest that was on the ground. She had laid her eggs there. A killdeer, in order to lead you away from her nest, will act like she is hurt. Since Oreo was near her nest, she fluttered away, like she was injured. But Oreo stayed where he was, waiting for me. The distressed bird changed her tactics and began dive-bombing Oreo, pecking his head, and making a lot of noise. She was doing everything she could to protect her eggs.

The mother bird, watching and guarding her nest, reminded me a lot of God. He is like that bird, watching over us and protecting us. The psalmist in the Bible describes that kind of protection:

> *"The Lord watches over you—the Lord is your shade at your right hand; the sun will not harm you by day, nor the moon by night. The Lord will keep you from all harm—he will watch over your life; the Lord will watch over your coming and going both now and forevermore!" (Ps. 121:5–8).*

ABOUT THE AUTHOR

I come from a long line of farmers. My grandfather moved his family from Montana in 1937 to Dallas, Oregon. I still live in the same house that he built on the same farm he first settled.

When I was five years old, I drowned and was brain dead for five minutes. After that day, I found myself struggling to relearn things that I already knew how to do, but couldn't do any more, like tying my shoes and walking. And, I still have problems to this day, with speech, reading, and spelling. My parents had me tested to find out why I was having a hard time understanding and doing things. While I was being tested, I was asked if I had almost died at some point, because that would explain why I was suddenly having to relearn everything I already had known how to do. When the testing was done, the doctors explained it would be very hard for me to learn things that others can do and that I would never understand very much. My mother just looked at them and said, "I don't care what your tests say, my daughter will do better than you say." From that moment on, my mother, who had studied to be a teacher, worked with me daily to help me understand things I needed to know and to learn as much as she could teach me.

As I got older, I saw how different I was and how easy it seemed for other people to do the same things that I struggled with. I accepted God into my heart at a very young age, so I trusted him and talked to him about everything. God told me all that I would be doing for him, though I wondered how a farm girl with such disabilities as I have could be that person for him. Then God showed me through my stories that if I accept my disabilities as a gift from him, I can be the person he wants and needs me to be. I am finding out each day that because I see things differently, I have a unique way of understanding things that has helped me be able to help others through my stories, which I enjoy sharing.

When I was in elementary school, they would have us write stories, which I really enjoyed. However, my handwriting was not very good and I could not read, but that did not stop me from trying to get my stories on paper. My mother would sometimes turn off the television when we were young so we could have family time. I would run off to get my stories I had written. I was so excited and couldn't wait to share my stories with my family, but they had a hard time understanding what I was saying as I struggled to read what I had written, so they didn't understand me or my stories.

I never thought I would be a writer, because in my mind, a writer needs to be able to spell, read, comprehend, and understand what they are reading, and all of those things are very hard for me. When God told me I was going to be a writer and share all of my stories I've written, as well as new ones, I told him all the reasons why I couldn't be a writer. He told me I just needed someone to hear my stories. God told me I need to be patient, honor him, continue to study his word, and pray for others. As I listened to all that God was telling me, I realized that I had learned all he had been telling me on the farm, and that is why God has chosen me to be a writer for this hurting world.

CPSIA information can be obtained
at www.ICGtesting.com
Printed in the USA
JSHW070750240523
42147JS00008B/288